I SPY

OCEAN

ANIMALS

WITH MY LITTLE EYES!

For Kids Ages 2-5

A

C

G

E

D

E

H

This Book Belongs To

_____

_____

_____

This book is especially
designed for the Ocean Animals
lover toddlers and
preschoolers.
It will increase their visual
ability, problem solving skills
and concentration.

Best Wishes!
- Azulan Creatives

I SPY with my little eye something beginning with...

A AND B

A is for

Angelfish

B is for

Blue whale

I SPY with my little eye something beginning with...

C AND D

C is for Crabs

D is for Dolphin

I SPY with my little eye something beginning with...

E AND F

E is for

Eel

F is for

Flying Fish

I SPY with my little eye something beginning with...

G AND H

G is for Goldfish

H is for Hermit Crab

I SPY with my little eye something beginning with...

I AND J

I is for

Islands

J  is for

Jellyfish

I SPY with my little eye something beginning with...

K  AND L

K is for Killer Whale

L is for Lobster

I SPY with my little eye something beginning with...

M AND N

M is for Marine Iguana

N is for Narwhal

I SPY with my little eye something beginning with...

O AND P

O is for

Octopus

P is for

Penguin

I SPY with my little eye something beginning with...

Q ... AND R

Q is for

Queen Conch

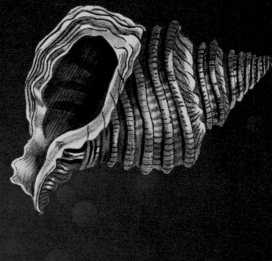

R is for

Rocks

I SPY with my little eye something beginning with...

S AND T

S is for Shark

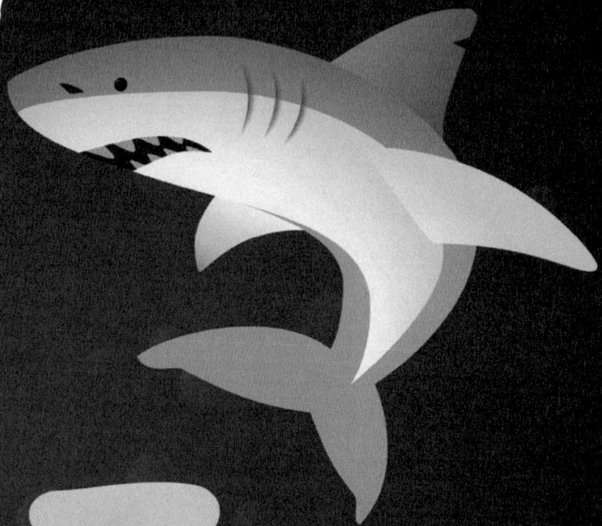

T is for Turtle

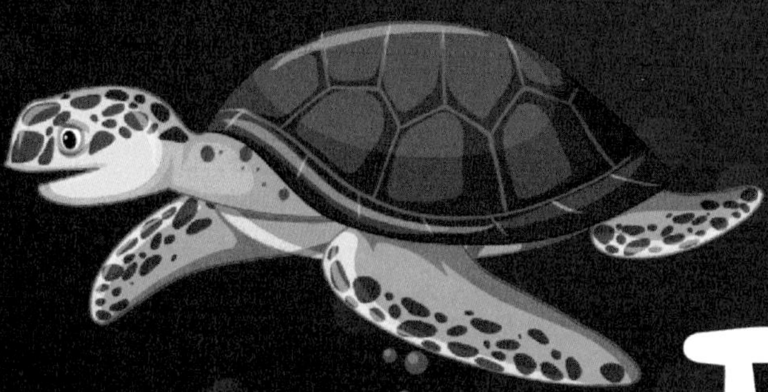

I SPY with my little eye something beginning with...

U AND V

U is for

Urchin

V is for

Van

I SPY with my little eye something beginning with...

W  AND X

W is for Whale

X is for X-Ray Fish

I SPY with my little eye something beginning with...

Y AND Z

Y is for Yellowfin Tuna

Z is for Zooplankton

I Spy 4 Missing Animals

I Spied 4 Missing Animals.

I Spy Biggest Animal

I Spied Biggest Animal

I Spy Animal in Red

I Spied Animal in Red

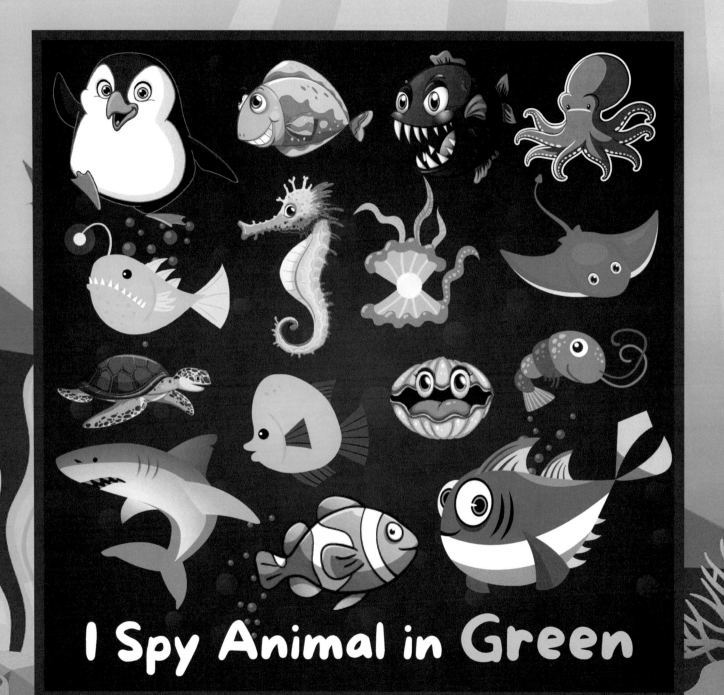

I Spy Animal in Green

I Spied Animal in Green

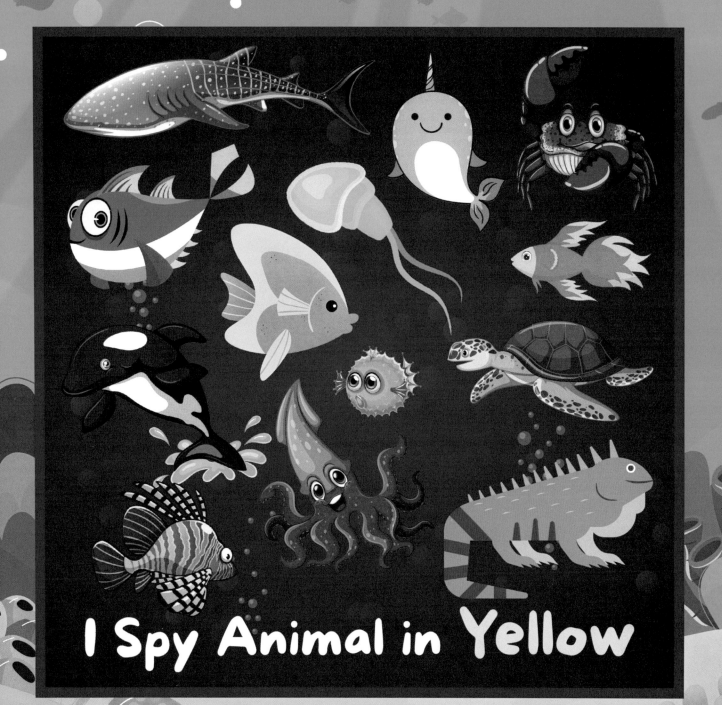

I Spy Animal in Yellow

I Spied Animal in Yellow